Poems on the Gate Post

Olivia Mulligan

Fisher King Publishing

Fisher King Publishing
The Studio
Arthington Lane
Pool in Wharfedale
LS21 1JZ
England
www.fisherkingpublishing.co.uk

Cover design from an original concept by Anna Wanczyk

For James – my favourite Yorkshire man

(sorry Henry, you didn't quite make the cut)

Why all the poems?

In April 2020, during the Covid-19 Lockdown, I received a letter confirming that I was in the 'at risk' group and advised to shield for 12 weeks. I packed my belongings into a bag and moved into the safe, sanitised bubble that is the home of my retired parents in a quiet North Yorkshire village.

My Mother suggested that I write a poem each day inspired by the self-isolation. She suggested that we then display each day's poem at the end of the drive on the gate for passers-by to read. "It might make people smile," she said.

I agreed to the challenge because, let's be honest, what else was I doing? I had already re-arranged my sock drawer three times that week and it was only Tuesday. Or was it Wednesday? Anyway, I didn't have a good enough excuse to not agree. I decided to leave a phone number for people to text in suggestions for topics for the upcoming poems, so the whole village could feel part of the project too.

At first, I took on the 'Daily Poem' task quite literally as that, 'a task.' Something to do to fill the time.

However, as the days went by and the collection grew,

it became so much more than that. Writing these poems became the highlight of my day. It was heart-warming to hear from the residents of the village, many who I had never spoken to before, telling me how much joy they received from reading them – I owe both my Mother and the 2020 Lockdown experience a huge thank you.

Now then. Kettle on. Yorkshire brew. I hope you enjoy reading the poems.

The Lockdown Clock

Lockdown clocks move slowly -
ticking and then eventually
tocking

tick
tock
tick to the
tock
I watch the clock
ticking
tocking

mocking our isolation
clocking our agitation
blocking our entire nation
from thriving.

"Wrong"
my mother told me.
"Embrace this time," she said.
Use it to chase your dreams
face your fears
place your priorities
trace what's holding you back
create space
for a space to learn.
Pause. Breathe. Slow down.
Showcase your passion.

Lace your days with writing
inviting others to read

uniting people with prose,
or even better:
Poetry.

We Locked My Father in The Campervan

Cocooned in a sanitised shell
he whistles through the window
singing with the starling
that's perched on the red brick wall.

Darling, darling, darling
it's not a Campervan.
It is a Motor Home.
Your Father is isolating in the Motor Home.

A giggle, a softened smile perhaps?
No humour intended.
This is a serious piece, capturing the essence
of our existence, through written word.

How absurd, that we have locked Father
in the Camper- nay, Motor Home.
Separate homes, dreaming the same dream -
of the day we can all roam free

and alive

Experimenting with Rhubarb during Covid-19 Lockdown

It's not just rhubarb
Said with the M&S voice
It's home grown pink stalks of succulent sweetness
Stirring endless recipes of choice.

Chopping on the kitchen slate
Spooning sugar and stirring smoothly,
Steadily transforming into syrupy
Rhubarb rose and almond muesli.

If muesli sounds too healthy
Let me tempt you to a brioche
Vanilla sweet bread with rhubarb sugar
Yorkshire rhubarb - oh my gosh –

That's good.

Lockdown means that Elevenses
Comes around about half past nine
Sticky ginger rhubarb flapjack
Served with brew and a clementine.

Beside a Yorkshire tea of course
Perfecting your baking abilities
Next up – the classic – rhubarb and custard
Thinking up many more possibilities.

Lunch is a fried mackerel sandwich
Served with a rhubarb coleslaw
For dinner there is too much choice
But with fresh rhubarb you are sure.

To start shall be a fragrant broth –
Vietnamese rhubarb soup
Slurped in isolation
Day-dreaming of your friendship group –

A recipe to remember when we're back to the family gatherings

Lucky that rhubarb is in season
Guess what we've got for the main?
Crusted pork chops with grilled rhubarb
Thrilled to be cooked again.

Again the fridge light sparkles –
Don't forget your pudding!
Tangy rhubarb tiramisu
With a side of clapping and thudding.

It's 8pm on a Thursday
And it's the music of lockdown cheer
Bashing rhubarb kitchen pans
With a wooden spoon – fighting fear.

Soon we will be together again
With rhubarb gin and rhubarb fool
But for now, please eat it alone
And obey the two metre rule.

What is wrong with you?

A poem by the dog in Covid-19 Lockdown

I won't wash my hands
I'll lick them instead
And then I'll lick you
And then I'll play dead

But don't you worry
I'm very much alive
One walk isn't enough
I'm desperate for five

Or six or seven or eight
Or a hundred
You've been acting strange lately
And I've certainly wondered

Why do you stare at a screen all day?
What's with all the clinical gel?
Why are you on the phone so much?
What gossip have you got to tell?

You're not exactly going out
You haven't waxed your upper lip
And your hair looks a bit of a mess
That could do with a snip

I don't care that you look a state
I'll still love you 'till the end
And I won't obey the two metre rule
Because I'm man's best friend

Home Schooling

In Maths we attempted fractions
Mum drank half a bottle of wine
She said it was from Bordeaux
So that's Maths and French combined

It seems Food Tech was cancelled
Because we ran out of penne pasta
English was cancelled too
So that the day was over faster

Geography has been postponed
Because foreign travel is denied
"What about rocks instead?" I asked
Collecting some gravel from outside

After lunch was Drama
Though I wasn't the starring role
Parents argued like Eastenders
"Who used the last toilet roll!?"

In Art we made new toilet roll
Prit-sticking Kleenex together
For P.E. Mum had good intentions
But sunbathed because of the weather

"Don't see the point in History," she said
"We're writing the books today"
For Music she continued to sunbathe
Singing 'Deja-vu' by Beyonce

It's three o'clock already
And today has been fun although

Perhaps I'll make a suggestion
That I'll teach Mum tomorrow

How Lucky We Are To Live Where We Do

Each day my dear friend
dreams of sunshine rapeseed fields and
feeling grass beneath her feet

Each day my dear friend
picks crumbs from the kitchen lino
from Paul – who she is yet to meet

Paul – who is practically a stranger
pays half the rent and
is possibly called Pete

Locked in a London postcode
trapped in a boxy bedroom
eleven floors up from the street

Each day my dear friend
stares through the narrow window:
the silent jungle of concrete

Each day my dear friend
dreams of Yorkshire rolling hills and
hearing the spring lamb bleat

How do I isolate?

(in the style of the poem 'How do I love thee?' By Elizabeth Barrett Browning)

How do I isolate? Let me count the ways.
I isolate on the phone, for my loved one's voice
My lobes can reach, when touch is not a choice
For my art of hearing and ideal space.
I isolate to the level of every day's
Most mundane, looking for light.
Seeing life freely: the day becomes night.
Seeing life purely, in numerous ways.
I isolate with video conferencing put to use
To isolate with loved ones afar.
I isolate with particles the air doesn't lose
With my body. I isolate with sorrow,
Smiles, chores, of isolation; and, if God choose,
I shall but isolate better tomorrow.

The Yorkshire Village Doctor

If I were a doctor
I'd prescribe packs of Yorkshire tea
Safe and suitable for all
It's like the Master Key

Unlocking a sense of comfort
As your hands snuggle the mug
Unlocking an inner joy
As you sip, slurp or chug

I'd start you off with Yorkshire
With a splash of milk
The colour of a Werther's Original
Tasting as smooth as silk

But not as expensive as silk:
Works out about three pence a bag
Cheaper than other prescriptions
And cheaper than a fag

You can use it recreationally too
When you want to impress a friend
Pressure's on though. Make it good.
A bad brew will certainly offend

Once you become a regular
You might like to try the hard stuff
Maybe Green? Mint? Or Ginger?
Or Rooibos if you're really tough

You might be reliant on tea now
Temporarily, your freedom is gone

But take it easy, take a breath
And stick the kettle on

Dreaming of Yellow
(a poem for the Yorkshire Air Ambulance)

I dream of yellow
Tulips and sun dresses and
Helicopters in the April sky

I awake to sunshine
Acrylic paint and an easel
As I paint yellow in clouds up high

I turn to learning
Japanese in an attempt
An attempt to pass the time

Helicopter becomes herikoputa
And 9am becomes 5pm
The time to clock in with Skype

We speak of yellow
Tulips and sun dresses and
Helicopters in the April sky

We speak of loneliness
Togetherness and last April
When a yellow helicopter saved her life

Curry From Scratch

Inspired by my politically incorrect Father!

Rolling, rolling, rolling
Rolling my chapati

Have ten if you're skinny
Have one if you're fatty

Flour here, oil there
The kitchen's looking tatty

Is it beef? Is it goat?
Or is it pussy catty?

Is it chicken? Is it lamb?
Or a roasted ratty?

Have no fear – it's veggie here
Lentils all the way!

Extra spice – make it nice
We're making curry today!

Finding Witches' Thimbles

The bluebell family gathering
huddled on the woodland floor –
more azure, more sapphire, more violet
than your eyes have seen before.

Pause.

Crouch to the carpet
of wild hyacinth too blue –
too blue to not be captured
by pixels that I'll send to you.

Look.

Sun-dappled through a macro lens
I squat to the cuckoo's boots –
rooting down to be amongst
the indigo forest fruits –

Stay.

I'll stay here a little longer –

Fifty-six thousand-one-hundred and sixty minutes

Nine-hundred and thirty-six hours,
since the lockdown began.
Captain Tom becomes a Colonel:
An inspiring 100 year old man.

Nine-hundred and thirty-six hours,
since the lockdown began.
A French man completes a marathon:
On his balcony he ran.

Nine-hundred and thirty-six hours,
since the lockdown began.
Jamie Oliver gives store cupboard tips:
What to throw in your frying pan.

Nine-hundred and thirty-six hours,
since the lockdown began.
David Attenborough assists with home-schooling:
Our Geography superman.

What have I done in this time?
Those nine-hundred and thirty-six hours?
My leg hair certainly longer...
But that's not a superpower.

What have I done in fifty-six thousand-
-one-hundred and sixty minutes?

I have taken each day as it comes.

I am learning how to 'wing it.'

Remembering The Mountains

I paint the pointed summits
exposed &
Strong
surely kissing the clouds
above the hummingbird's song –

I sing about silhouettes
of mountains
snow-peaked over emerald lakes

Inspiring;

day-dreaming;

day-dreaming to be awake –

I mimic the minarets
of mountains
on my left ankle with a tattoo
reminding me of
You
& where we used to climb –

Me Old Man

"Y'don't get owt for nowt
y'know, y'know, y'know."
S'what me old man used t'say
t'me and m'sister Jo.
"Ow do my son," he'd say
with his voice all gritty and low.
"Get kettle on and make us a brew,"
he'd say t'm'sister Jo.
"Eee by gum, you're growing lad;
you'll be on farm soon y'know.
You'll be strong enough after winter
when we're clear o'this bloody snow."
I were always me old man's favourite.
Oh and he weren't afraid to show,
cos he called me sister useless,
in bed with her heavy flow.
Me Mam said he were dead chuffed
when they 'ad a boy y'know.
They went out t'Thirsk t'celebrate
as me Mam 'ad that pregnant glow.
Poor Jo doesn't mean t'be useless.
She doesn't mean 'arm y'know.
She's dead gud at makin' bread dough n'that
and o'course she knows how t'sew.
Boys thought she were a reight bobby dazzler,
a reight gud sort, although;
me old man only cared for farm n'such,
not sportin' a pink ribboned bow.
He were dead chuffed when he'd worked dead 'ard,

even in that bloody snow.
Y'know me old man never stopped workin',
even with frost bite on his toe.
"Y'don't get owt for nowt
y'know, y'know, y'know."
S'what me old man used to say
t'me and m'sister Jo.
That were before he popped his clogs.
He's dead, y'see, y'know.
Lying low beneath Yorkshire earth,
below the grass he used t'mow.

Let's Learn Some Facts

Lockdown is the perfect occasion
To learn some obscure knowledge
Seems we could all use some brain power
Making up for missed days at college.

Did you know that a lions roar
Can be heard from eight miles away?
And did you know that heart attacks
Are most likely on a Wednesday?

Did you know that Golf Monthly
Pay the highest journalist salary?
And did you know one hour of golf
Burns 500 calories?

Bet you didn't know that in Denmark –
Owning a Guinea pig is illegal.
Their Queen requests caviar for breakfast –
Oh how very regal.

Documents say pigs were the first
To ride in a hot air balloon –
Then they allowed a cockerel
And then a Yellow Baboon.

9% of Americans think
Chocolate milk comes from brown cows...
And did you know that in Thailand
Marshmallows are not allowed.

Here's one about the Antarctic
And the vast amount of ice –

5% is penguin urine
which has identical molecules to mice.

Did you know that those facts above –
I planned them... to mislead...
I made them all up to spread a message:
Be careful what you read.

Self-Isolation VE Day

Black and white photographs on my screen
I screenshot and I scroll
"Not victory of a party of any class –
Victory of the British nation as a whole."

I Google 'British cake' recipes
To contribute to the celebrations
Victoria sponge seems the favourite
So I'll make enough to feed the nation.

But alas, it will just be me
A VE party for one
But with good spirits I'll put up the bunting
I'll still cheer and sing the song.

I'll surely be singing on FaceTime
To my next of kin
Together we'll sing 'We'll Meet Again'
Echoing Dame Vera Lynn.

The Struggles of a Video Chat First Date

I wore a sexy turquoise top
And a trendy matching scarf
He would never have to know
About my shameful bottom half.

Winnie-the-Pooh pyjama bottoms
And leg hairs of a gorilla
All he saw was my immaculate make up
Smiling as sweet as vanilla.

Speaking of vanilla that's what he was
And by vanilla I mean BLAND
His profile said 'adrenaline junkie'
And that he 'played drums in a band.'

It said that he 'loved to travel'
And that he had a 'Masters in Aviation'
But all he spoke about was the virus
And what he'd been doing in isolation.

Alright, give him a chance, I thought
What hilarity had come his way?
But "Today I completed a puzzle"
Was all that he had to say.

I waited for the punch line
Whether that be laughable or profound
But instead – a breath of silence
And in that awkwardness we drowned.

He could have at least turned the question
And asked what I'm about

And then with passion and enthuse
I'd say "absolutely nowt."

The WiFi connection was strong
But the chemistry: not as desired
So if I were Lord Alan Sugar
I'd be telling him: You're Fired.

Please Don't Forget

History books will be written
For our future generation
The documentation
Of Covid isolation

Pondering the psychology
The ultimate exploration
The journey of the mind
The behaviour of the nation

How did the nation unite
When two metres divide?
They danced with their heads
Their minds amplified

They danced with pixels
On a screen in their hands
They spoke with strangers
Because strangers understand

Life after lockdown
Shifted temporarily
They kissed a little longer
They smiled unnecessarily

Then their to do lists grew
High-speed trains returned
Hustling, rushing, pushing
Forgetting what they'd learned

Let us beat the history books
For we have the power to write

Let us write our own journey &
Let us always see the light

Teetotal Prayers

Some days my heart feels heavy
For those on the Front Line
For those in Intensive Care
And for those who didn't survive.

Some days my heart feels helpless
For the loved ones left behind
But then I remember my role in Lockdown
My job is to be kind.

It is my mission to write Poetry
With the hope to make people smile.
I'll write Limericks and Haikus
And I'll keep them all on file.

Some heart-felt, some humorous,
But mainly anecdotal,
My next one titled 'Spare a Thought
For Those That are Teetotal.'

Seriously though. Imagine that.
In Lockdown without a drink.
Everyone's feeling anxious and
The whole world is on the brink.

Indeed, let's pay a huge thought
To those on the Front Line,
But let's also pay a little thought
To those without a glass of wine.

Rainbows On The Glass

Red faced kneading bread from scratch
Scratching Yellow chalk for a hopscotch match
Matching Pink pyjamas during home schooling
Schooling with Green crayons in our kitchenette learning
Learning to eat more Oranges for vitamin C.

Seeing the world a little more slowly
Slowly realising that bluebells are Purple
Like purple pixies singing
Singing for the sky so Blue.
Singing 'I can sing a Rainbow,
Sing a Rainbow,
Sing a Rainbow too.'

Those Were The Days My Friend

I attended the village school
with my lunchbox and plastic spoon.
The teacher said, "enjoy these days –
for they'll be over soon."

Fifteen years on, I'm here –
and now I'm twenty-five;
remembering the days of burgundy jumpers
and how very hard we tried –

to not hear the playtime bell
meaning playtime had come to an end.
We'd line up in a zig-zag fashion
driving our teacher around the bend.

We'd bend the rules so sweetly –
secretly sending notes in class –
secretly plotting our hide & seek tactics
as we daydreamed through the glass.

"To the top of the field and beyond!"
Is what Izzy and I would shout.
Joined at the hip at primary school –
friends for life, I have no doubt.

The teacher was right in what she said –
our school days were over soon.
We recall the days of clock-watching –
for playtime freedom at noon.

Where are my classmates now?
Besides 'adulting' and owning a car?

Cameron is now a Tree Surgeon
and Rachel works in HR.

Izzy's completing her Masters –
She'll have a certificate to show it.
I write poems every day,
but I can't say I'm a Poet.

Keep Making Music

The crescendo of the kettle
recently Dettol-ed to squeak –
squeaking clean –

peaking to a boil
slurring to recoil –
applause.

Pause. Take a sip.

The duet of tea and tongue
is silent.

During the silence:
You'll feel old
You'll feel young
You'll pluck thoughts from your head:
A song unsung.

So sing?

Sing without judgement
without judging too soon –
you're off beat
you're out of tune

who cares?

Sing.

Sing out of tune.

Sing about coffee, the microwave or
the moon

Sing about singing –
being heard and being seen.
Sing about our lives today
cocooned in quarantine.

Write Something, Anything

One doesn't need war wounds
Or love letters in lockets
One doesn't need certificates
Or money in one's pocket

If you can see light in the dark
And sculpt shapes in the light
If you can play with possibilities
You can certainly write

You do not have to be right to write
And you do not have to be heard
Paint words to ponder, to discover
To be incorrectly absurd

Or correctly absurd
If that's what you choose
Write with your stomach, your heart,
Write with nothing to lose

One doesn't need approval
Or heavy intellect
We write to taste life twice
Taste the moment, taste retrospect

Let's write to taste life twice
In poetry and in prose
To survive we must share stories
So let's see how our story goes...

Hashtag Unprecedented Times

News reporters inform us
Of these unprecedented times –
Now everybody's favourite word
Which to me is quite the crime.

'Unprecedented' in the work emails
'Unprecedented' Facebook posts
"Mummy, not in these unprecedented circumstances..."
The seven year old school girl boasts.

Now unprecedented challenges
Navigating the Covid epidemic –
Which, in itself is unprecedented:
Now an unprecedented pandemic.

Can they not pick a new phrase?
Uncommon? Beyond compare?
Unparalleled and unheard of?
A bloomin' global nightmare!

'Unprecedented' sounds intelligent
As if you know what you're on about
But the very definition of the word
Means you know absolutely nowt.

We use the hashtag 'unprecedented'
On repeat like a Covid chorus –
Here's a plan – let's ditch the word
And hashtag, 'Buy A Thesaurus.'

Mr Whiskers Relocates to The Shed

It was a standard Lockdown evening –
I was enjoying my beef stroganoff.
Then my peaceful evening disturbed –
as I heard a suspect cough.

My cat spluttered in the corner –
a fur ball I suspect –
at least... I hope it's a fur ball...
it's too late to call the vet...

Cue frantic Google search
thanks to my hypochondriac persona.
Does my cat have Covid-19?
Does my cat have Corona?

Mr Whiskers continued to cough –
so I said, "look, I'm sorry mate –
I don't care you're a cat, rules are rules.
You'll have to self isolate."

I'll Get This One, You Can Get The Next

Danke to Munich
for birthing the Biergarten
in the year of 1812;
Oh how a beer in the breeze
puts modern life at ease
with companions surrounding oneself.

The rotting tables
and the fly-away coasters
indeed are all part of the charm;
Patrick is sloshed
as 10 of us are squashed
on a 6 person bench arm in arm.

Posh ones serve appetizers
and the beer ain't cheap
but we gathered there for Pam's 65th ;
We wore our best frocks
oblivious of the clock
as Lispy Len said "Give usth a kith."

There'd be belly laughing
there'd be hiccups
we'd be mocking and being mocked;
But at home we stay
awaiting Boris to say;
"The Beer Gardens are now unlocked."

No Water No WiFi

Once upon a time,
lonely,
shrivelled bodies gathered,
each morning,
to feel the freedom of water
to feel the warmth of a sauna
on crusty joints riddled with stories –
telling stories to fellow swimsuit strangers
now not strangers at all.

Once upon a time,
widowers
wore swim hats and smiled with dentures

changing into dry clothes slowly;

prolonging their journey home...

Today,
lonely bodies without WiFi
wait behind walls

waiting;

holding their breath through lockdown
as the swimming pool locks its doors.

You Know You're a Runner When...

When 'you're crazy' becomes a compliment
and 'foam roll' becomes a verb...
You'll leave your phone at home
to ensure you're not disturbed...

Undisturbed by a phone you run
run to think, or not think at all –
The dream is to feel a euphoric high –
The nightmare: to hit the wall.

You know you're a runner when
at least one of your toenails is black
pressing against various shoes for
cross-country or tarmac or track.

When you hear the phrase '5 mile run'
that actually sounds quite cathartic –
you get giddy when you think of speed work &
you don't laugh when someone says 'fartlek.'

You know you're a runner when
PR doesn't mean Public Relations –
but a Personal Record, a Personal Best –
the result of strength and determination.

The phrase 'it's all downhill from here'
sounds like music to your ears –
But the thought of a week off running
will fill you with dread and fear.

You secretly practice your 'arms up' pose –
crossing the finish line...

You'll run round in circles in front of your house because you can't end on 4.89.

SPF is Your Friend

We Brits be slave to the sacred sun
Taking as much as we can hack
Once a plum, you're now a prune
And there is no going back...

Some men feel the urge to remove their vests
Having their nipples on display
Their chalk white skin reflects the sun
And we don't have the nerve to say

"Please put that back on. It's April."

The t-shirt tan is a staple
Something we show off to our friends
An aggressive line of red and white
Where the sun damage starts and ends.

And not just minimal damage...
But damage to our largest organ
Sorry to burst your summer bubble
But our skin is just too important.

Indeed soak up that vitamin D
But remember that the sun is shifty...
The power to heal and the power to hurt
So wear your factor 50.

Yes enjoy the warmth, wear your shades
Eat ice-cream, eat frozen banana
But don't enter lockdown as a grape
And then exit as a sultana.

The Lockdown Ocean

In lockdown
We are like mystical ocean molluscs
Floating through the unknown –
The waters that nobody knew

Like a Great Pacific Octopus
Reaching into nine brains –
Our knowledge waits in a queue –

Two metre love from three hearts –
Frontline love and blood –
The blood that is blue.

Locked down, we explore multiple brains
Locked down, we nurse many hearts,
Loving voices and loving strangers and
Loving our loved ones, oceans apart.

Stay Just As You Are –
You'll Be Fashionable One Day

The lockdown mirror judges
My bushy eyebrows grow thick and long...
I Google monobrow fashion –
Is it right or is it wrong?

In 2002 a woman asked:
Does my bum look big in this?
"Of course not darling! Not at all!"
Her friends would surely dismiss.

Yet in 2020 the big bum is 'in'
Having a flat bum is quite a disgrace.
And remember a time when freckles were ugly?
Now models will paint them on their face.

Remember when the ginger kid used to get bullied?
She's now a fiery and fierce trend-setter.
And once upon a time, true beauty was pale
But now the deeper the tan, the better.

It used to be weird to have blue hair
But now it's beautiful to be wacky...
I read being skinny is 'so last year'
And showing 'too much' cleavage is tacky.

Perhaps varicose veins will one day be trendy
And we'll want more wrinkles than our Mother.
We'll praise crooked teeth and double chins
And when one boob's bigger than the other.

Still we diet, we bulk, we cover our face

Afraid to be different or wrong...
But everybody has a different body
And everybody was born to belong.

In for a Bumpy Ride

After 12 weeks
Leaking

The vulnerable

Into supermarket aisles,
The overcrowded nature reserve &
The buzz of the golf course

Because of course 12 weeks
12 weeks is different to 11 weeks
11 weeks and 6 days.

At 12 weeks we will pray –
Pray that we avoid an NHS wreckage
As we hear new news –
The new 12 week message:

Stay alert
Control the virus
Strap in your Nanas.

Just a Number

spaghetti hoops on toast
in front of the telly
tell me,

what even is an adult?
a middle aged adult
in the middle
maybe –
we don't know –
much about anything really –

really enjoying
wearing those dinosaur leggings –

egging you on
for a toothy smile.

smiling with laughter lines
lacing your face

facing each moment
in the moment
more freely than those younger years –
you bounce
inside candyfloss socks
your warm cheekbones blush
like cherry jam
prawn pink lips upwards
towards daylight stars –

What a Beautiful Building Site

My new practised and favourite pastime
Is watching the Builders work –
More amusing than the television –
Behind my grimy window I lurk.

I watch them and repeat my mantra
To focus on positive thoughts...
My lush green view is no more,
But I refuse to be distraught.

I repeat that bricks are beautiful
And that dust is a work of art
Head banging drills are a symphony
And by 3.30 they'll depart.

Yes they began at 7am...
But nobody likes a lie in.
Everybody loves a building site.
Don't worry I'm laughing, I'm not crying.

I'm not upset that I'll be overlooked
The new neighbours might be super...
Even if they have all night parties
I'd never be that party pooper.

I won't miss that field of green
I won't miss the peace and quiet
I'll force a smile through the double-glazing
To the building site racket and riot.

No Knack for the Brack

Bake to shake vocal chords
Oooing and aaahing
Opening the oven door
To see my cake
(Take two)

Too burnt was the first one
And take two, she's no better
Just wetter
With her soggy bottom...

Bottoms up for the taste test –
As predicted, she is raw
But maybe we'll enjoy
Slurping our wet cake through a straw?

I do my best to save her
Suffocating with buttercream –
'Tis the art work of a toddler
And a stab to my self-esteem.

I'll leave recipes to Grandma
I'll leave baking to Aunty Beryl
For my fruit loaf is too dry
And my fairy cakes are feral.

But I'll still join the baking front line
Together – a well oiled machine
Grandma does biscuits, Beryl does cake
And I'll be the spoon licking Queen.

Tomorrow is a New Day

Your garden must be immaculate
Bet your house is spic and span!
Not at all – filthier than usual
Still not washed last night's frying pan

My bottom is glued to the sofa
As I watch the dandelions grow
Contemplating tidying up
But then there's nobody I would show

I dwell on my festering antics
And my streak of inactivity
Physically I'm quite the slob
But I've honed in on my positivity

Positive that today I feel negative
As negative thoughts chitter chatter
Chattering positively negative thoughts
When nothing is really the matter

Except the stand-still world of lockdown
Unsure when isolation will end –
Waking each day to be cliché and mopey and
Longing for the voice of a friend

Living Next Door to a Building Site Part II

I take back what I wrote in the Part I poem
With all the building site positivity
For yesterday we heard the bird song
During the bank hol inactivity

No bulldozers and no earth shaking
No hurricanes of grime and dust
Just visions of overpriced new builds
Ambiguously 'detached' and 'robust'

Cruising in at sunrise
Wearing their hard hats, their crowns
Working hard and earning good money
As our house price plummets down

But let's not dwell on finances
As we drown in the noisy labour...
Let's just take a head shake and a tut
At how we never signed up for new neighbours

We'll reminisce of when we had sunlight
Beaming through the conservatory glass
Now blocked with built up brick work
On the field that used to be grass

Our postcard field of green
Will be a memory that we'll share
Taking the stillness for granted
And how we used to stare

At nothing.

Realising our house was once nothing
This house then shockingly new
Diggers and chaos were once here
Our home was a building site too

Perhaps it's not total destruction
But new life for a family
Aye. The building site is what it is.
And what will be will be –

I wonder...

I wonder if I wander there alone
Unknown eyes will stare, watch to harshly judge
Judge my feet on the public paths of stone
Sharp eyes reflect my purpose as I trudge

Heaving my lockdown legs up hills I'm free
Blood moves to circulate and rinse the doubt
But car-park eyes they'll soon latch onto me
Cold critique of my Covid whereabouts

I too critique the man with watching eyes
My rambling thoughts will question his desire
Our woodland wishes watered down with whys
With bitter thoughts of others we conspire

I long for pine tree shadows without shame
Perhaps my unknown stranger feels the same

Is It Over Yet?

shhh, she's shielding

cushioned in a mansion,

or a shed

shaving less frequently
frequently shifting

fridge to bed

bed to fridge

shhh, she's shielding
shut under a ceiling

shrinking speech
increased feeling

dealing with sunshine
shadows through the glass

surely shielding
this too shall pass

Like Listening to a Friend

The company of waves from audio
Music and speech dissolve our silent gloom
A stranger's voice that we now seem to know
Perhaps recorded from their living room

The song that takes us back to ninety-three
In California on route sixty six
Driving to drive, top down and feeling free
Forgetting that our lockdown life exists

When music ends the speech must start once more
Expect repeating news like garden weeds
Instead ear drums hear light of lockdown war
The unknown caller calling of good deeds

Music, weather and chit-chat from the phone
With radio I know I'm not alone

Mixed Messages

Watch the news daily
But don't be engrossed

Social media detox
Or twenty minutes at most

Work on your life skills
Perfect that lamb roast

Apple crumble for one
You're not allowed to host

Host dinner on zoom
For your daily social dose

Practise self love
But please do not boast

Go outside
But not to the sea coast

Wave to the post man
Disinfect your post

Learn to slow down
But don't burn the toast

...And if you do burn the toast
Then it's ok to cry

Because lockdown is lockdown
And emotions are high

Self-Isolation: A Haiku

The lockdown Haiku
Five – seven – five syllables
Is this a cop out?

I believe so yes
So I will give you three more
Making four Haikus.

The Lockdown image
In seventeen syllables
Is indeed a task.

Tasked to isolate
With WiFi and tighter jeans
Birdsong is brighter.

The City Commuter

today people are speckled
like winter freckles
not   too   close

heads bowed
in prayer position
worshiping

remembering

before

squashed under a stranger's armpit
huddled
yet alone
heads bowed
in prayer position
worshiping their phone

Greener Grass

Today the rain fell
Falling neatly on thirsty ground
Gently drowning, the petals swell,
Smiling sweetly to a drip drop sound

Today the rain kissed
Happy tears into rivers dry
Dribbling Life's plot twist –
Grass is greener on the other side

Tomorrow the clouds be grey (again)
Dappled with chill in June
Chit-chatting neighbours will surely say
Enough rain.
We want the sun back, and soon –

The Lockdown Conversation

Oh hi. Hiya. Y'alright?
Oh. Mute. You're on Mute.
I can't hear you.
MUTE.
Maybe it's my compute---
No. Nope. It's yours. It's you.
MUTE.
Maybe try and restart? Or...Reboot?

Oh. She's gone...
Looks like it's a video chat for one...
So might as well ramble on
A little solo liaison
A chance to expand upon
The current lonely situation...
Chit-chatting to myself, for the duration
Just me myself and I, here in isolation
The blank screen consultation -
My lockdown conversation...
Hi.
Hiya hun.
So in this lockdown... What have you done?
Have you learnt any skills?
And have you begun
Your to do list?
Have you cycled? Been for a run?
Have you learnt French just for fun?
Have you done a tonne
Of DIY and each day thought,
I HAVE OUTDONE my pre-lockdown self!!!

Erm...

No. Nope. Not at all.

The answer is no.... "Hun"

My to do list... I haven't begun

I've not done a tonne of housework

I've just a tonne of eating

Packet pasta.

And no. I'm not any faster

Cos I haven't been for a run

Or learnt French for fun

Cos I got bored at 'un'

And the only thing I have outdone

Is my... online shopping habit...

Now the owner of a lizard

And a dwarf rabbit.

Yes. I have certainly spun

Out of control.

... Control...

You see that's something I lack and –

Oh!

You're back!

Hi.

Hiya hun...

What I'll Tell My Grandkids

Back in my day
We had a public gathering ban
I couldn't visit me Nana
And I couldn't kiss me Man.

Back in my day
Loo roll was like gold
We panic bought dried pasta
As if we'd never been told –

Other food groups are available.

Back in my day
Our hair and beards grew long
We practised 'Staying Alert'
Without a definitive right or wrong.

Back in my day
It was safer to be alone
Too risky to have celebrations
Birthdays were on the phone.

Back in my day
First dates were held on Zoom
Quarantined couples were make or break
Hence the Lockdown baby boom.

Back in my day
Forced to move at a slower pace
We realised the meaning of love
Longing to be face to face –

The Winners' Waiting Room

Behind closed doors, stable doors are open
Yards to be swept and manes won't comb themselves
Lungs fire up each day to keep the hope in
Wild hearts will race for trophies on a shelf

Ears pricked to when the bets are placed again
The grind of lockdown hours will soon be shown
Silks are worn to sweat with the fine champagne
Awake at dawn to peak and then postpone

The sunrise grooms, they cannot work from home
Four legged colleagues cannot mix their feed
A prized possession cannot freely roam
Born to race, the race is their only need

Their chocolate eyes will watch the pearly moon
Dreaming of gold, post lockdown, racing soon

A Big Lockdown Birthday

Little Timmy woke up 'a man'
It was his birthday – the big 'one – eight.'
His friends still call him Little Timmy
Because puberty showed up late.

But quarantined friends were non-existent
No friends to celebrate –
Instead a slice of toast and a handmade card
From Dad and Step-Mum, Kate.

"I know you wanted a personalised bike –
but now I'm furloughed that's a big ask...
so I thought that this would come in handy –
it's a personalised face mask!"

"Thanks Kate," said Little Timmy,
"Here's to a wonderful year!"
"Enough of this cheery nonsense!" screeched Dad.
"The boy needs a god damn beer.

Poor lad having his 18th birthday
Without a pint or short in sight.
Don't worry son, we'll take you out –
Clubbing under the kitchen lights."

Lockdown metamorphosis
Meant the living room became The Crown Inn,
The Dining room became The Black Swan
With bottles of Bourbon and Gin.

Little Timmy didn't like the taste
But appreciated the imaginary pub.

Dad and Kate liked their drink
And soon it was time for the 'Club'...

The disco smoke machine was a hit
And it came from the kitchen kettle
A white wine spritzer too far
Kate was bopping to the heavy metal

Squat dropping on the kitchen table
The role of 'parents' had disappeared
Timmy snuck out the 'club' to call his friend:
"Mate... things got seriously weird..."

How To Hug

How to hug in 2019
Remember that old chestnut?
Remember that muddling minefield?
When you want to hug someone but –

Societal cues are baffling
Some identify as 'not a hugger'
Hugs are different for different people
Your Gran is not your lover

We learn the hugging subgroups
Is it friendly or romantic?
Is it joyous or are they mourning?
Are they skinny or gigantic?

Is a hug appropriate?
Or will a hug insult?
Do you consent to hug me?
Or is this an assault?

How long is too long? We often ask
Is there a cut off time?
Can we hug strangers on the bus?
Or is stranger hugging a crime?

'The 'Parenting' chapter is the easiest
Hugs for bedtime, hugs when proud.
'Hugs in 2020' - the shortest chapter:
'Hugging is not allowed.'

I Like Some Things About Lockdown

No more limp handshakes
No more high heels
Slippers and dressing gowns and
Home cooked meals

Less congestion
Less money on fuel
Less money on everything
Cos non-essential's not cool

More time for resting
More exercise too
More time for artwork
More time for a brew

But time can be sneaky
It can be painful and long
Long lists for lists' sake
Emphasising what's wrong

The internet is still slow
The news is still depressing
Bills must be paid and
Politics is distressing

People still chew loudly
Late people are late for zoom
You'll still have to pay for shipping
And you'll still have to tidy your room

Confined and claustrophobic
Unable to spread our wings

Big problems might be bigger problems
But we'll enjoy the little things

My Search Engine Friend*

*This started out with me innocently typing in 'How do I...'
into *Google, intrigued what the most frequently asked
questions are. You can see the results in the poem below:*

How do I get an antibody test
How do I use zoom
How do I cancel Amazon Prime
How do I make room
On my iCloud?

What happens when you die
What happens when you quit smoking
When you block someone on WhatsApp
What to do when someone is choking

How many litres in a gallon
How many deaths today
How many cases of Coronavirus
How much does Beyonce weigh

How do I convert pdf to word
Convert ounces to pounds
How do I write a daily poem

Sorry, no results found

Sitting on The Fence

awake to make to take to fake to break

i can't i won't i shouldn't but i might

await the state update the fate the hate

i can't i won't i shouldn't but i might

i will not write the poem
                              that i do not want to write

What Does Freedom Feel Like?

Freedom is like glitter –
a sugarcoating on the brain –
like galloping on abandoned sand –
salt crystals through your mane.
It's nostril breathing forest air,
toes touching ocean terrain,
it's whistling with the birdsong,
it's flying without a plane,
it's candy-floss at 5am,
it's belly laughter pain,
it's remembering your last kiss,
but knowing you'll kiss again.
Freedom is the sunrise,
it's running through warm rain,
releasing your recurring dream –
you're free from the knot of shame –

Confession

Confession:
I murdered a poem
brutally.
But it was already dead
when I strangled
scrunched
buried it in the bin
suffocated with yogurt pots and
yesterday's rice pudding tin
that should have been recycled

But it didn't deserve to be recycled.
It didn't deserve the time.
It mocked rhythm and insight.
And it didn't even –

What's that word –

Rhyme?

I hoped the ball of litter
would thud and
smash!
into the bin
like a heavy ornament breaking
killing poetic sin.

Instead it flew gracefully
like a dandelion sphere blown by a child –
a snowflake handmade by lilac clouds –
like origami in the wild...

I killed a poem that was already dead
and the death was quite pathetic.
But the act of killing an atrocious poem,
somehow became poetic...

Couch to 5K

My eyes workout to television
My spine sinks to slouch
Here I'm doing what I do best –
Sitting on the couch.

I understand the pillow politics
I understand the Law Of The Settee
I understand 'The Chair Life' and
'The Chair Life' understands me.

My friends, they don't understand me –
One of them had the nerve to say:
"Why don't you get off the sofa?
And try the Couch to 5K?"

Well, the bum-cheek cheek of it!
To give up my sofa routine...
(I assume that's what they're suggesting)
Though I don't quite know what they mean...

Do they think I'm strapped for cash?
That I need some money in my hands?
I really don't want to sell my sofa
And it's definitely not worth 5 grand...

But by 5K, they meant 'distance'
And by 'distance' they meant 'jogging'
Apparently I sit down too much
And my lungs – they need unclogging.

I clarified I could keep the couch
Then I hopped on the fitness bus

The guidelines suggested 'comfy trainers'
But I didn't really see the fuss...

Lesson one: Don't mess with the guidelines.
My Crocs did not suffice.
My settee cradled my blistered feet,
Shins caressed with packs of ice.

I learned many lessons the hard way.
I learned some men need sports bras too.
I learned jogging speeds up your digestion.
I learned the hedge will become your loo.

I like to head nod to the other joggers.
I like to sprint the last 50 metres.
I like running when it stops.
Because my sofa feels even sweeter.

The Sounds of Lockdown

A 6AM silence
like the hushed breath at a memorial
a birdsong tutorial
a trafficless editorial graphic on the roads
leading to your home
where the kettle is louder.

Prouder than yesterday
for touching your toes
hearing meditation melodies
hearing your breath through your nose

your bare feet play music
on the creaking floorboards
leaking more chords of
peace and noise and

what is that noise?

A strange man is downstairs -
I can hear his voice
voicing instructions without giving choice.

My Mother chooses to listen
to the strange man's words
masking the silence: the song of the birds.

His voice is priest-like
like a clear cut cube
the strange voice speaks
through the window of YouTube –

to my Mother and many, his own lockdown army

the lockdown thumb twiddlers, learn origami

my mother folds and refolds
old shopping lists
crunching the paper as the strange man insists –

Enough of that!
I close the door,
opening the window,
for the silent encore...

Forgetting If You Forgot

mourning
   the forgotten

cups of tea
   chilled

on a crusty coaster
   that you thought you'd cleaned

definitely
   thought about cleaning

but didn't

definitely will do that
   on Wednesday

which is tomorrow
   or today

   or yesterday

yesterday's tea
   is still there

still cold
   liquid toffee

mourning
   yesterday's tea

   forgetting

   it was actually
   forgotten
coffee

A Naked World

Imagine if nude was the norm
If people wore clothes for a dare
If covering up your bits and bobs
Would encourage neighbours to stare.
Bare feet, bare legs, bare bottoms
Topless top halves with no shame
Nude is nude and naked is naked
And nobody looks the same.
Some will have more jiggle
Some will have more hair
Imagine if nude was the norm
If people wore clothes for a dare.
If jumpers were embarrassing
If trousers were just plain wrong
Imagine that mortifying moment
Caught in public wearing a sarong.
Imagine the 'special' swimsuit beach
Where children are not allowed
Imagine a naked London
A skin showing naked crowd.
Skin to skin and nipple to nipple
Squished on the rush hour train
Rushing into the naked city
No anorak for the heavy rain.
Accessories are controversial
Is it acceptable to use an umbrella?
A man once wore a hat, you see
And made history as Strange Hat Fella.
Imagine if nude was the norm

If people wore clothes for a dare
Only your other half would see the clothes
And even that was rare.
Imagine a naked Vicar
Never wearing a robe for prayer
Imagine giggling as a child
About what clothes she secretly wears.
Imagine naked picnics
Having dinner with your naked Nanny
Walking free in your birthday suit and
Showing the world your belly button.

For My Father

Sun from seventy years
in his skin
resembling his morning coffee
or a toffee
which he's not allowed anymore
because the dentist said so.

Stories from seventy years
on his tongue
tap-dancing around the kitchen table
able to twist words into an outline –
a silhouette
of industrial cities
or a mountain
counting other mountains to pass the time
climbing for the climb and
for the stories.

Reading thoughts from seventy years
in his mind
to find
a particular sculpture –
his daughter
knowing that he taught her
the art –

silently
teaching her the art
of determination

Overcrowded, Overpriced, Overcrowded, Overpriced and Repeat

bacteria clustered on the bus
you're flustered
muffling a cough
shuffling to exit
at the next stop
disperse –

stop   for a take out coffee
take out your purse
in a shifty café queue
blend in –
be shifty –
queue to queue and
spend £3.50
(3.50!?)
for a cappuccino trend

£3.50 for a cup of milk froth
in your own reusable sloth mug
stood in single file
from the barista who didn't smile
far from worthwhile
but masking your sorrow
you'll be here again   tomorrow

Summer Solstice

self isolating for three months
is like winter –
the slow time between Christmas and New Year
    but less turkey on the plate
    more birdsong in the sky
singing the same song each day
stuck on a loop
looping to repeat –
repetitive strain
of making tea

repetitive phone calling
repetitively calling people out
repetitively using the word unprecedented
repetitively using a garden trowel, weeding,
repetitively weaning yourself off the biscuits
repetitively napping
repetitively googling symptoms
googling what is in store today

today
today is going to be a long
day
daylight galore,

the sun rising at 4.43,
staying,
setting at 9.21,
16 hours and 38 minutes of
day

the longest day
the sun standing still
still shining
still offering
light
offering
meaning

meaning
winter is coming

The Calm Before The Storm

the mist wears a jacket of mist
missing some bits, where sunlight speckles through
through the kitchen glass
ingesting the morning view

morning oats are sprinkled with rainfall
pouring cinnamon sugar from a spoon
soon spilling sultanas on the counter
distracted by the daylight moon

distracted by the daylight, distracted by –
the dog at my feet
distracted by pinging emails, pinging microwave porridge
and kiwi pips in my teeth

cod liver oil tablets bounce on floorboards
towards the dog's wet nose
bulldozing his tongue over golden pills
still barking at my toes –

must put a pound in the swear jar
and replace 'F-ing hell' with blimey
must replace panic with positivity
at least the dog's coat will be shiny

Problem Not Sorted

Meditation is free
almost –
it's free for 30 days
and then you'll have to pay for the App –
pay for Jeremy's voice –

"Just breathe"

"Just breathe"

"Just breathe"

those words make me seethe,
     I hold my breath.

What Jeremy doesn't know won't hurt him
     but I might.

His feather light tone ripples through veins
     like an echoing tomb
scratching my skin like an itchy perfume
patronising my rush hour head

     SHUT UP.

shut up with your   "a thought is just a thought"
I know it's a thought because it taught
me   to   think
your voice is annoying

annoying imaginary clouds and breath work   resumes
with force I pray
for Jeremy in the room,
with me,

so I could thump him
    dump him from my morning routine
and alas,
he stops.

Now I can pretend to enjoy my day
pretend I don't have a problem –

Nine Until Not Five

Where would your childhood footsteps want to go?
Enchanted forests whisper in your ear
Touching trees to be running free, tip-toe
To a new world – of nothing, disappear

What does your adult head voice say to you?
Send that email and work on the weekend
Work evenings, meal times, repeat, then re-do,
Live to work, work some more, and let's pretend

Things are ok – alright – not bad, you say
Insomnia is common, so that's fine
No time for reading stories through the day
After moonlight meaningless work deadlines

Where would your childhood footsteps want to go?
To find the paradise you didn't know

Summer

Can you feel that?
- It's summer
Butterfly wings flutter
Floating backstroke
Through the breeze

Can you feel that?
- Twenty six degrees
Sunburnt knees
Covered by a cloth
Protecting picnic scotch eggs

Can you feel that?
- It's summer
The buzz of the drummer
Humming bumble bee chords
Towards
The adored summer sun

2020 Bingo

Ready for a bit of silliness?
Grab your pen and grab your specs
It's the 2020 possibilities,
what on earth will happen next?

New rules on public transport –
no smiling and no talking
But holograms on phone devices –
ultimate social stalking

University fees triple –
oh wait. Already done
Let's triple them again –
for future debt filled fun

Another planet is discovered –
this time this one's flat
Another species is uncovered –
the pedigree rainbow cat

Fake news has become worse –
... or has it?... Nobody knows
Some be true, some be false –
just to keep us on our toes

There's a new social media channel –
'Look At My Ordinary Life'
A new movement called Manhoodism –
#NobodyNeedsAWife

The house prices sky-rocket –
people turn to life at sea
Research shows caffeine is deadly –
so no more drinking tea

But sugar is good for you –
so let's make the world sweeter
The vegans have become cannibals –
eating the meat-eater

There's a new café to buy a husband –
it's called Donor Canteen
There's a pandemic global lockdown –
that's Covid 19

Full house! Full house!
Said the voice of a fool
But there is a Full House Ban –
there's a six person rule.

Life Advice

Perhaps they ran out of bubble wrap
In the year of 1994...
"Toughen up, lass," my Dad would tell me,
"Ya can't come second in a war.
Pain is just a weakness leaving the body
I've told you this before
It's not the winning, it's the TAKING APART
And ya can't come second in a war."
My debut egg and spoon race
Didn't quite hit the mark
Last place, sweat on my face
I was so slow it was almost dark.
Maybe she's not a winner,
But an explorer, my Dad thought,
A Father-daughter adventure hike –
Waterproofs and maps he brought.
Military marching and heavy lungs
With cliff top drops below –
"Don't be a wimp," my Father told me
"And don't eat yellow snow."
Advice continued from his lips –
Not exactly life saving,
More - *"Don't wipe your bum on a broken bottle"*
And *"Never push your Granny when she's shaving."*
I now look back on his advice
The silly words that Dad would say –
His tongue-in-cheek words made people smile
And silly words can make someone's day.
I write this poem as if he's died –

Nope. He's still the same as before.
I wave him off to his Seniors Golf match –
"YA CAN'T COME SECOND IN A WAR."

All Pudding No Sausage

I lay the kitchen table with an extra place –
My friend Julie's coming for tea.
Mum's in the shed as Dad starts to cook
Cos they're all about equality.

I joke about the role reversal:
Soon he'll be wearing a dress,
Mum will be having the lads around
And Dad will clear up the mess.

But enough about them, more about Julie
My friend Julie's coming for tea,
A merry, joyous, dinner time
With four instead of three.

"So where's Julie from then?" asks my Dad,
"Did you say that she's Bulgarian?"
"No, she's British, an old school friend.
She now works as a Librarian."

"That's the one!" He says as he chops –
Chops the onion into dainty slices,
He then lifts the cling-film from the meat -
Marinating in juicy spices.

I watch speechless, as he slices the meat
Like last night's TV – 'The Caesarian'
How do I tell my kitchen-proud Dad?
That Julie is a vegetarian!?

"So... Non-Bulgarian Julie...
Julie the Librarian...

What does Julie do for fun?"
"Dad. She's a vegetarian."

Just like the TV drama –
Dad faints as he drops the knife
Then Mum shimmies in, in her overalls
As I try to bring him back to life.

Never turn down CPR training –
Dad splutters to explode
"We cannot serve non-Bulgarian Julie
Hole without the Toad!!!"

Her arrival time was fast approaching
As a family, we began to mourn...
"Plan of action. We'll smile and lie.
Let's just tell her it's Quorn."

Oh How British

again
stand at the window
(inside)
for fewer drips of rain
sip sip
sip
the steaming brew – cup in hand –
cup-free-hand on your hip

again
sigh
a British sigh –
wonder why
the washing wasn't brought in
wonder when
the rain will stop
wonder who
ate all the custard creams

My Friend, Anxiety

Three months is ninety one days
(that's a quarter of a year)
full of could haves, would haves, should haves
having to spell out the unclear.

I could have grown a third of a baby
and you'd have thought so by my new tum –
but that's just due to lockdown nibbles
and sitting on my lockdown bum.

I would have done more housework
and cleaned more hairs out from the drain –
but I was too busy with busy thoughts,
busily being insane.

Is that word still allowed? Can we call someone insane?
Because I identify with that description, locked down with
my hectic brain.
Anxiety they call it - the tornado has a name
claiming your sacred head space
and burning a blistering flame.

Just calm down and breathe, they say.
Like your breath can put out the fire.
Sorry my Fireman's furloughed
so I'll stay stuck in this barbed wire.
Sorry I meant 'Firefighter.'
Old habits die hard, you see.
Man or woman, they're not here.
Isolated: it's just me.

Three months of isolation

the time has come: I'm free.
Fire brain survivor for ninety one days –
I think I'll add that to my CV.

Three months of isolation
the time has come: I'm free.
An anxiety sufferer, firefighting daily but
saved by poetry;

Unleashed into an anxious world –
I could - I won't - I might –
I might not remember to breathe –
But I'll remember to write.

ACKNOWLEDGEMENTS

Thank you to my Mum, Carolyn – for her ongoing love, support and for always putting up with my nonsense. Then thank you to my Dad, Tom – for never putting up with my nonsense... for his brutal honesty, for teaching me the art of determination and for his wonderful cuddles.

Thank you to the residents of Dishforth Village, North Yorkshire, encouraging me to keep writing. Thank you for stopping on your daily walk to read the poems. I would sneakily watch you scan them from the kitchen window, but couldn't quite make out your reaction. I hope they made you smile.

Thank you to Marjorie, who lives across the road. Thank you for spreading your positive and determined attitude – "THESE POEMS JUST MUST BE MADE INTO A BOOK!" According to Marjorie, there was no other option. It had to happen. Thank you for suggesting that I do a crowd-funder to raise funds to allow me to turn the collection into print. I didn't think anyone would really want to donate, but to my astonishment, they did.

Which leads me onto thanking everyone who so kindly supported the project. Thank you to Kathleen, Shelia, Tess and Eddie, John and Beryl, Tom, Carolyn, Marjorie,

James, Inge and George, Helena, Andrea, John, Rosie, Mandy and Nigel, Ty, Beth, Lorraine, Caroline, Anett and Simon and Kim, Christine, Sue, Sam, Jackie and Nick, Venetia, Sue and Dicki, Lydia, Frances, Hayley, Tessa, Heidi, Liz and Mark, Paul, Eamon, Adrian, Ann, Bertie, Martin and Christine, Izzy, Brian, Adam, Rachel and Tim, Deb, Carolyn and Mike, Connie, Elizabeth, Cathy, Molly, Minskip Farm Shop, The Allerton Players, Esther, Monika and Mike, Maisie, David, Tanja, Tania, Deborah, Lisa, Steve, Anne, Zoe, Alice, Ann and Malcom, Lindsay and Andy, Mike and Lotti, and Annie. I can't thank you enough for your generosity.

Thank you to my friends – you know who you are. Thank you for your sweet, heart warming encouragement for me to keep writing and keep sharing the poems. Especially to the friends who hate poetry but said the poems have made them smile. You guys are my inspiration.

Thank you to Harry Whittaker from BBC Radio York, for putting my spoken word poem 'The Lockdown Chat' forward to the BBC Upload Festival, to be aired nationally... I certainly didn't expect anything, but, Yorkshire me Pudding!, it was chosen! Thank you to all of the team at BBC Radio York for such wonderful kindness and support, inviting me on the show several times to ramble about the daily poetry project.

Thank you to poetry legend Ian McMillan, Bard of Barnsley, for so kindly responding to me when I sent him the sonnet, 'I wonder.' He recorded a video of him reading it which he then shared on his social media. Hearing those smooth Yorkshire vowels read-out-loud the words that I had cobbled together was certainly a pinch me moment!

Of course, thank you to Fisher King. Thank you for publishing my first poetry collection in book form. In fact, my first anything in book form.

Last but not least, thank you to James. For loving me from a separate household (during lockdown) and for never getting tired of telling me, "not long now" every single day for almost four months.

THANK YOU...

OLIVIA MULLIGAN

Olivia Mulligan, or Liv as she is known, was born and bred in North Yorkshire. After spending several years in London, completing a degree in Drama and Creative Writing, and a short spell working in the city, she could no longer resist the call of the Yorkshire Dales and so returned to her roots.

Liv is a keen cross country runner, a coffee barista, and now – poet. Her spoken word poem, 'The Lockdown Chat' was aired at the 2020 BBC Upload Festival in the Writers' Tent.

"I have many childhood memories of making up and performing silly rhymes, songs and stories, even before I started school. These days I find I am inspired with poetry ideas when I am out running. I can't jot down the verses until I get home so to help me remember the lines I keep repeating the words out loud as I huff and puff up and down the Yorkshire hills, sounding truly insane.

"I love how poetry encourages rebellion, experimentation, freedom and so much more."

To keep up to date with her poetry antics, follow Liv on Instagram & Twitter: Liv_Mulligan

www.ingramcontent.com/pod-product-compliance
Lightning Source LLC
LaVergne TN
LVHW010305070426
835508LV00026B/3435